T0272993

Some Beheadings

Some
Beheadings

Aditi
Machado

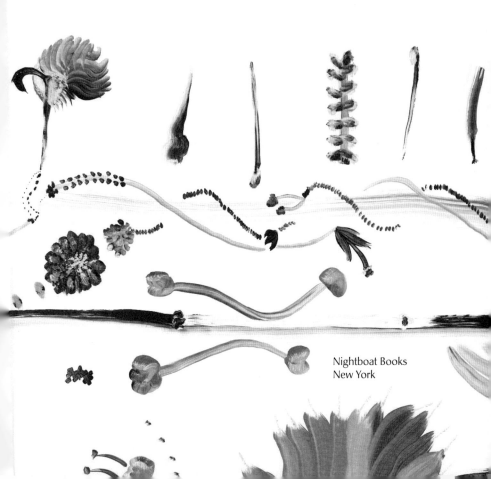

Nightboat Books
New York

Copyright ©2017 Aditi Machado
All rights reserved
Printed in the United States

ISBN: 978-1-937658-73-1

Design and typesetting by Margaret Tedesco
Text set in Christiana and Electra
Cover art: Thomas Kovachevich, *Backyard*, 2016.
Courtesy of the artist and Callicoon Fine Arts, New York.

Cataloging-in-publication data is available
from the Library of Congress

Distributed by University Press of New England
One Court Street
Lebanon, NH 03766
www.upne.com

Nightboat Books
New York
www.nightboat.org

CONTENTS

PROSPEKT

Every day I wake & my life
is private. I see a sun. A coiling
memoir. There is anaphora
in the sun. There is a sun,
it has brightened. A loss in this
unyielding every day I wake —

there is privacy. A mirror
brightens the fascist
in me. When the speech
is made the proscenium
erects everyday
theatre. I make a kind
of debris. When I speak
the fascist in me speaks.

O countries & natives, o
wordless obeisance, o privacy
coiling in the memoir —

a great book I will write
is not my private life. A tornado
is simply warning for nothing
that appears out of chaos. A sun

in the fascist, in the hard cold
private life of the citizen, I
make a breakfast. There is a sun
still. There is a house
I move through. A bracken,
a tongue meet.

A bracken, a tongue.
A bracken, a tongue.
A tongue, a tomb
I move through
to arrive at word-like
edifice. Gingerroot,
canna, asparagus, iris.
There is a room
I cook in. There is a
sun outside it.
I empty a vase,
I fill a bowl,
floral notes, spice.
The throat is a corset
I wear, I tighten,
from which I exude.
I eat, I speak,
it is sexual. Prep
work, like eros, is
in the minutiae.

When one enters a room one becomes its audience. One audits its dimensions, decides whether to reverse the dynamic or keep it. If one keeps it one remains that most mysterious of facts: a furnishing. One sits in a corner & one reads, deity. If one reverses it one turns into that most gratifying of agents: a speaker. One expends energy, loses one's reserve. The most minimal sculpture is a rock. The work of privacy is maximal. Look at this, draw some curtains, exit.

Breakfast makes time
out of edibles.
When a body desires
its continuance
that is need.
When it desires
its dissipation
that is want.
I make an order.

Felt in the mind of god is an idea.

As god I write my book of ideas.

'When the universe thinks itself without being outside itself, we name that "thinking" God.'

When I think myself I do not disappear.

When I think my thinking my thinking disappears.

When I think myself thinking I onan.

It is the opposite of what they say:
the gods do not equal their occasions.

There is a speech
under the speech
as below the sea
more sea.

For Piaf there was
singing & the wind
covered it.

There is a body
& a sexual body
& the kiss was
to the first of these.

There is a speck
moving along the river
as along the edges
of a room.

There is a dance.
The interminable leaving
of rooms for which
there are seasons.

& there are gods & there are species
& faces & windows & clouds & copulation.
One of the world's patterns is collective.

A wind, a text.
A wind, a text.
The wind touches
to the skin textile.
Rayon, a cotton tag.
To be in public,
to feel private.
I am watched
& pleasured.
Grateful, I return.

One day there are notes you follow in an orchestra of worldly movement, the next you skew. The propagandas come into play when you become aware of how you are against how you never are. What are the alternatives? Consider the continua that are vegetal & mineral. How they be you cannot be. You breakfast, you organize. Futures in the distillery. Pasts in the windmill.

So wind is a textual experience. So I revel in its ambiguities.
So may I stand whole minutes suffering its arrivals at the station.
So may I in this manner feel felt in the mind of whatever
is greater than I. & in the consideration of what is greater than I I
become lost in the folds of eros. & in appearing out of this maze
I become ready to speak my name to the stations that ask.
This is always & everywhere how I am sculpted, baroque
& wavering, submitting my shape to some common stipulations.

My shape, a desk.
A desk, a window,
a lighting condition.
To breakfast
amid the books.
There are events
to be lived through
that calcify
as required,
thinking conditions
to be sipped.
I am tired & sleepy.
The taste of things
does not resurrect
grand palaces,
stretch-marked
memory.

Events collocate bodies. The copula is
witting. It nests toward death, chooses to requisition
via tongue, unpierced, uncut.
I'll cut it when I want to know more.

Unpierced, uncut,
unpruned, uxorious,
remaindered satin-
like, in prophecy
washing, in acid
washed.

A garden, a pattern.
Worms & tongues.
Sexual organs, peeling
green parts, fruit
& thorn & thorning paths.

There is a garden I garden.
A bracken, a tongue meet.

One day there was no organization or I could organize nothing & there was radiance, a rare radiance from within, of saws & metal in the hot works, a floral incertitude moving like decay & something about speaking to myself was unlyrical & unspecial, so deeply private that

I were an I wending the garden, I there way out there
picking flowers in the heat. I were subsuming an ornamental
floral convention until it were entering were vaginal
until something like sap were vocable & I readable,
pathlike down the way, lovers everywhere
& upon the knee, no clauses.

A thing is a cicada when it tends toward sexual disorientation
& I is an orient in the sense that all things wend toward me.

'Pain is a flower,' its symmetry

opens radially. The sick flower,

'a sort of diffuse, bodily pain, extending

by radiation,' I never find its center.

Every day I wake I see sun,
it's blue. I wake, I see wine
glass. Through it
its other side. Something vital
in me is worsening
the problem. I believe
like memory. That is,
when I remember that is
prayer. To make one's mind
religion is deep pool-
like monomania &
there was a snakebite
in the dream. Through it
its other side. Pain
when I wake. & to worsen
the problem into its full pasture,
why pain when I wake,
the bite in my thigh as if true.
When prayer is to remember,
when mind is to religion
I confuse the effects of limbs
for limbs & through the sheet
the sun is blue. Disproportion
is a labor I achieve.

One way to see grammar is to think fields, how bare they are until you look underneath. At their limits are nouns to which you run & you pick them up & cannot.

The Speech:

I spoke as in a wheel
spokes.

Supported the curvature, I
supported the ongoingness,

the goingson, some
beheadings, I

& the fascist in I
on the dusty road

reinventing.

O copular scapular,
o joints & weddings,
your presence, your
prescience, this love
of grammar I cannot
resist, this day
that will not pass
its morning, this soft
labor, delicate palate.

ROUTE: THICKET

GRACE, EXCESS

I

Is there a sublime, that's my birdsong today.

Is it immanent, that's why I wrote a page I doubted.

Slipping on questions
all questions are gloves against rancid weather
gloves being grace.

Grace, I think.

Grace, I think I can feel it as image.

> (The white of sheep
> invades a field.)

Grace not of but as
god, that unusable concept
used in excess.

II

Look into excess.

Watch that wanderer
watch him seed his grotesque plants. His eyes become
the vines he becomes.

Do I want an image with which to think asks
is matter abstract grit
a way to open up open up.

Or do I want to touch something so I cease.

Watch it cede
like bamboo in the bamboo grove.

Do I want to listen in the grove so loud
the grove becomes a loud speaker
a lyric wet.

That is a sublime that is
immanence an excess an incest a prosperity a bloom
isn't it.

NO, BUT

A pause, a shrub.
I look, I prune
the recession,

dip, & think
no.

A shrub on the lowly
bland plain — I

tend it to
attenuate it
& think no.

Forget volta,
find its
opposite

is thicket.
Attend it.

Attend attention
as you would pause,
materia medica.

Attend thicket,
it breeds
its own

interruptions,
tarries & turns
so that you don't.

'I am my land,
expressed' & expression.

Attend thicket
as it thickets
as I

& expression
forget rifts.

No thistle
but overthistle.

PASTURAL

How express
a rustic thought

how when
everywhere

ruminants
lie grazing
& still

clouds
you thought.

How in an
unpasture
of endless

say beauty

were you to
pose

fanfare
on your head

horns delectable
mind
stamped out.

Say you
want to say
your cud

to whom
will you.

How amid
the image of cows

can you not
be them.

Back to it
ruminant.

Back to your
remnants.

This picture of cows
is the rust
of your mind.

Ruddy light
ruddy trees
ruddy path

winding
you
up

singing
*I was born
in a barn*

were you.

You make
a made place
you were

born in.
You bring up
your bolus

a red lozenge
the color
of barn

under a blue
pastille sky
chewed.

Bring it up
travel your
internal

backdrop
unsettled.

COMMA

The white of sheep
invades a field,

a circle empties
into another circle.

A PLACE

In a film a blue sky
is grey & joins me.
Sensorium equals

mind, voluptuous
signal composed
by hill & quiet

in the hill-bell.
In a grey sky
the film

& the coming
to a place is

sometimes
enough
& even more

is the coming
to it
as sheep

from a point
to the right,
from within

a thick of pine,
this coming upon,

the white of sheep
invades a field,

a circle empties
into another circle.

IN THE WEEDS

I had thought to tell a tale but between having had & having thought
a plant fell out from within the crease.

I thought to have green fingers but I move so abstractly.

I am thinking now to describe what it's like to touch something.
What it is to rub off on someone.

When two matters interact should I hope to keep my skin.

Ambling in the wind, lost in perfections, those blips
along the odometer of time, my feet in the weeds—

my head capitulates to them. Little plants, little events. That's how

I think. A decapitation, a lovely guillotine wind lays my mind
in the weeds. That's how

I touch a plant. My water touches its.

ROUTE: WESTERN GHATS

LEECH COUNTRY

As within the raucous meditations of high priests you find yourself moving and trepidatious and in the far black moving black trees. For once when I say you I mean you, the morphology pristine. You may not think there is anything particular to you but you may also not think. Somehow volume is more believable when the leech makes love to you when you deplete. Many days go by undoing the central leitmotifs of your life. You have no nature, only wilderness. This is what it is like may not be said. This is what it is not like neither. You take your apophasis and your deliquescence and when it rains like this you have felt everything. Petrichor, petrichor, you call, wishing for a way to always be seed.

HILL STATION

The top of this hill is called a viewpoint but is not figurative. We've made a philology of it which is immaculate which is as we now are, figural. Lemongrass on the slopes grows wild wind through it. The trellises are in place, the fences called eyes. There are rivers in the distance that milk. And we graze and check the motorcycle as it stays upon the slope. And we grow wild on the point through the downward sloping lemongrass and the notional. There are moments in which the condition of the mind approaches the condition of the body which we call ecstasy which now occur.

Somewhere deep darkness is parapet to acts of survival. The strangler prospers in this heat multiplying its arms. As one who does not who listens who analogizes who is the analyst of events so quickly occurring as to be historical what is left save to be consumptive. It is rich and my prolific hands alert. There would be berries, there would be wood. Finite oneiric reflections by the water by the trees straining light. I agree on the premise

of the forest. I agree on the appropriate sounds asphyxiating. Somewhere deep language sexualizes its horror over how it may be infiltrated is body where speech is movement and all you can do is move. Somewhere deep

giddiness is lux and air which I need air and light like poverty disappear. And the choker like an aroma surrounds like ornament sits. And to be giddy you must have eaten you must have breathed. There are berries and there is wood. No passive recipients in a peaceful and phagous world.

Something inwardly:

SPEECHES, MINOR

infinite rose
peeled & bliss.

I walk as if moving will evaporate as if scent.

Discomfort moves in the body like discourse
between sea & moor:

the bad weather turns terminal.

I think toward the sky & the bellies of underground

creatures. This makes a dense paragraph of mist. Inside mist what you see is neither truth nor untruth but discussion rising into dissolution.

« In a kernel I admit
I am deeply

but have not yet found
my apathy. »

Sun bounces off railway tracks:
ancient ritual of geometry.

By the tracks opens a flower:
refrain.

The flower is general & particular & ancient.

It satiates the erasure of a palm.

There is a richness in saying everything we know.
There is a richness in saying everything, we know.

The flower has opened a disparity in the earth
that is granular: refrain.

In the medial moments like a closing couplet I said one thing and then another into a coliseum or seashell:

« I think of feeling as an act of purity. That I wind through cornfields and feel rustlings is incalculable. Though I have acted out of purity I have not felt thought. Thought is not open to me though I sense it from the edge of a field watching the horses and the horses' masters. I have not been a slave to kindness. I watch horizons like blades. I watch the gorgeous animal of movement and its whip. I watch the gorgeous plant of movement and its whip. I cannot tell time without the whip. »

The whole village was there, minus its people.

ROUTE: DESERT

A wind blows, the desert unfolds.

To sleep on its pillow is succulent as cacti swelling in times of plenty shrinking in drought.

When I lived in the desert I was so young & spiny drinking rain into my lungs. Now it is culture everywhere & specular.

The desert melts, the sky's glass.

I muse on this as on myriad crystalline forms.

The cactus flower prescribes water, its bouquet wafts
along the coast of an absent sea.
Sand divines my desiccation. So too with culture,
words I use to speak my distance from the desert.
Culture too resides in me an intercourse most internal.

Sand flares, I parse the granular

the heat valorous. Opening its sepals

rain palsies. A navel in the sand

elements an oasis. In the steely night

lying on my belly. In the steely night

lying on my back.

'. . . on the sand,
Half-sunk, a shattered . . .'

A neck spills its faint lesson, the hour glass fills with lust.

What is heard, what is not heard congregate on the sleeves
of weather rotating the windmills.

Materials survive, soaked and running, formic on the rocks,
Opheliac in the pool.

The listening I was summoned to perform, I perform it.

In heat my eye fears what seduces my ear.

Voices stem lush, sink like petrol.

Laborious, ambulatory desires turn the desert.

Here is a romance pointing *here, here*.

In heat my tongue delivers a sermon like a caress.

In heat your tongue delivers a sermon like a caress.

In the heart of the desert a decadence
My arrival   its catalysis

labial
dunes

runes

Inside looking
like outside looking
sways.

Sand in a grey
photograph
pointillates.

Grey soils
approbate
grey singing.

The pure bird
of no negation
arrives.

Feelings drive
an arm toward
fruit.

Things to say
then happen
in a spasm.

Things meaning
soil & finger
shape a line.

A circus tents
a circle
in passions.

A cactus
circumscribes
water.

I touched someone
in that desert as
time won't.

BLESSED IS

A day, avid
centuries.

A time when when
bestowed locus.

I look about the place
as it dislocates

for the venereal heart.
Here

is a symposium
& time is ludic.

I feel I am happening
in a sleeve.

Locusts are swarming.
Lust is. Here is

a valence. We were
paragraphing the sun.

My friends & I, unhappy
with anything pitched

higher than darkness,
discouraged beatitudes.

What is more dangerous—
perfection in the body or
perfection in the mind? I saw the seashell

everywhere making a unit of life,
the unsprung sound
of a thing unseen.

There is a place in my heart.
There is a heart.
There is my academy

hinging the preposition.

I configured myself one day by not
entering the pool. No contentment
overflowed.

To fill my life as an index,
to feel crying as by onion—

there is an astringent for everything.

It is lexical.

Blessed is the heart.
Blessed is my gethsemane

of florid logic. I am lucid
in the afternoon.

Graceful living—benevolence,
pure bawd.

ROUTE: MARIENBAD

When at night there are facts I would speak as if water
I would spill

I turn to curvature silken

as in pyretic. Pollen forewords the night.

When reading is sleep, speech turns action into passive reception of the cornerstones I go beyond, the cliffs sharpening into profusion. Assays made into such dense imagery, in which I bear to move, heat the kiln. That is, the objects emerging from a night of deep sleep—extreme listening in which the mind is a honeycomb—equal the manifold foreign literatures I've been nursing.

'Walking is hard labor'; 'Walking is the exact balance of spirit and humility'; description is epiphany.

The moment I describe my day to myself as if I were perambulating through infinite foliage, a tender frottage the opposite of claustrophobia; the moment I fall asleep obeys a literary convention I touch, explaining its features to myself; 'absolute contradiction seemed at the heart of things and yet the system was there'; I sink into another elegant counterpoint.

'Restraint, dreams, restraint.'

Between Marienbad and the distant ocean
a single baroque animal

opens a pomegranate. Ancient colonies
of ancient civilizations spill out as red beads.

'That we sleep plunges our work into the dark.'

Sometimes I work through a problem in sleep.

Most often sleep is a problem phrased I cannot.

In the dream I'm lost, a maze in the body of a rat.

In the dream I'm bitten by a snake when I wake.

LIKE THINKING LATERALLY SLEEP POSTURES.

Night bus. Odd,
necessary
circumcision.
Circumlocution.
The way a thing
moves, yields
to its passengers.
Half-sleep,
bitumen—
darkness of roads.
Impenetrable lights.
Billboard of apostasy.
Extrusion of leaves.
Purity of signal.

A thread occurs in my botany as rudiment and delicacy. A stamen bears pollen. I stand firm. The root grows into a trunk grows into a branch: the stem grows into a stem grows into a stem. In the sky's red canopy the thread warps an occasion. The way I somnambulate city weeds are phrenic, like the oldest languages telling me where to stop for sense/direction.

TO READ A SENTENCE FOLLOW ITS
GRAMMAR TO THE PRECIPICE FROM
WHICH IT LEAPS INTO SOMETHING
LIKE TOTAL SURRENDER TO A REM
CYCLE.

TO MISREMEMBER SLEEP LET THE
DREAM PERSIST. THAT IS, WHEN THE
BONES IN YOUR FOREARM SPLIT IN
TWO, KEEP THE FRAGMENTS AND LET
YOUR HAND DO FOUR WORKS.

The bed, its roundness. Among its
terrors waking into man. Waking
into ant-like seriousness. Dreams
do not disturb one's senses

of humor, do they? Quatrains.
Decisions of equal temperament.
The sleep is going away to a corner
of the system so it can be awake.

Waking into wounded body is less
terrorizing than how wonderfully
six a.m. windows of dark light.
The one fully awake individual

is sexually involved. A casement
for the involution to be regarded.
Nexus of glorious morning alarum.
Sleep and speech. Creeping

of sunny days back into the pocket.
To speak means how much
wakefulness? Want for iron-cast
commitment to this investigation.

Dormiveglia, commas are
dreams. Can you wake up
from a sentence like
you wake up on the porch?

'Those who sleep poorly seem always more or less guilty:
what do they do? They make the night present.'

When at night the woods burn
toward a gold of rolling fields
fallow light does what eyes do
turned inside out. When at night
the curvature warms itself facts
spill into blue sheets, sinewy
as the one going under them,
explicating fire as figure for
what must die in order that inner
become outer: the wrought
manners in which I say I fell
asleep and don't know how but
the sheets were warm and I felt
a mild decadence, an explicit
industry as that of bees.

I SLEEP AND WAKE AND SLEEP AND WAKE AND
THIS IS PROSODY.

As I begin to believe in materials less as textile and more as touching everywhere is a kind of terror or lust. There are six minds employed here and the sixth is the least ephemeral and substantial.

As I attempt to extricate myself from the sheets I make a place like a deep place in water, sound moves as it should. Through these strata some diagonal light, dry trapezoids. White questions flare, aging dandelions.

PROSPECT

Like a street I become
as I walk it, the agent of walking
as if blood on the lip, a kind
of hunting in which one eats
prior to capture, I perceive
an arrow, the arrow turns in
on itself, o complex
presentiment. How long before
I walk into the sea remembering
what the kelp felt like: like felt.
I think a line into the future
but on the sidelines history
is pressed along its pleats. I think
the period is a decimal point,
I dare not be more precise. I think
I'm not human, I'm grammarian.
There was a future, the future
passed. So a will was there,
now there isn't.

TORSO

I have been lying here under a meniscus.
Beside me there have been some burials.
I have been asked to think & I do & I refuse
to be for the moment. I assume a perfection
of time that displaces my whole sense
by which I mean my whole intellect
so I can look upward & say I have been
lying here under a meniscus. I have been lying
next to some burials & I think what I have been
asked to do is say where the future is
as if it were hidden like calculus from everyone
but the elect. You turn your eyes to the past
is a figure. You turn your eyes to the future.
Time is tense in speech or how I speak to you
is tense as you lie farther away from me
than sound can carry. I cannot tell which side
of the meniscus I've been on but I have lived
is a way of saying something ceased.
The dead ones because I believe them lie
for me & the grass that grows above them
billows & the weeds are weeds I would
bind myself in. The future is full of suspense
& here is the banal: every thought
I think billows & the weeds continue
so where am I but always moving into
the prophecy a second ahead. I cannot tell
which side I'm on. Do I, am I
filtrate? I turn my eyes. Meniscus, turn.
Been lying here too long. My torso hums
a lowly plain. The waveform wreathes a tree.

ARCHAIC

I thought this was a way a new way.

I wanted to call it human.

Speech! Speech! it's been wept before.

It was a work to stand in the sun that erosion.

What is regal is pain is pain legal?

Speech? After each time I lost the right under a legislature so commonly verdant.

Speech? The only way is to turn outside turn into an outside. There a lip.

A lip at the end of town not the seashore.

A new way I kept thinking a new grammar of replacement not I I'd rather be spit.

Standing on my lip like a promontory standing archaic.

Standing on my lip like a promontory why this staging why these dark

lines of surplus harmony these elastic expenditures such supernumerary stars?

So I could speech I needed the staging of mouths opening like kinds opening all kinds of meteors.

Something opened a space for me but I'd asked for time so long planets so long plants.

Then I spoke a spoke.

I spoke a sentence and ye took offence.

I thought a new way burnished make that.

Irresistible propaganda.

I have nothing new for ye but an ancient latticework I rot.

IF THOUGHT IS

If I am alive

If I am thinking
nothing has stopped

in the way of wheels
I cannot leave

If where I was born
was a basin

Where was it
I was thinking

If I breathe
If the wind

If resilient
the basin

is cold
& thinking

tensile

If thought is life
& the want

of thought is death
the incendiary dress

NOTES

'Prospekt' quotes from Etel Adnan's *Sea and Fog*, Robert Creeley's 'The Flower,' and Marcel Proust's *Le Côté de Guermantes* (translation mine), in that order.

'Route: Thicket' quotes from Edmond Jabès's *The Book of Questions: Volume I* (translation by Rosmarie Waldrop) and relays a scene from Robert Bresson's *Au Hasard Balthazar* in some sections.

'Route: Desert' quotes from Percy Bysshe Shelley's 'Ozymandias.'

'Route: Marienbad' quotes from Susan Howe's *Souls of the Labadie Tract*, Gary Snyder's 'The Etiquette of Freedom,' Iris Murdoch's *An Accidental Man*, Tomas Tranströmer's 'The Journey' (translation by Robin Fulton), Lyn Hejinian's 'My Life,' and Maurice Blanchot's *L'Espace littéraire* (translation mine), in that order. The poem refers obliquely to Alain Resnais's *L'Année dernière à Marienbad*.

'Prospect' makes reference to the title of a painting by Kazimir Malevich.

'If Thought Is' uses language from William Blake's 'The Fly.'

ACKNOWLEDGEMENTS

In the monsoon of 2014, I spent three days in some dense and biodiverse locations in and around Sakleshpur District, India. This led to the composition of the three site-specific texts included in 'Route: Western Ghats.' I am extremely grateful to my brother, Siddarth Machado, and his fellow researchers for their hospitality and ecological wisdom during this time.

Versions of these poems first appeared in *The Capilano Review*, *February: an anthology*, *FOLDER Magazine*, *Hardly Doughnuts*, *The Offending Adam*, *Poor Claudia*, *Volt*, *webConjunctions*, and *Witness*. I am indebted to the editors of these publications.

Thank you to CJ Martin and Julia Drescher for making a beautiful, letterpress-covered chapbook out of *Route: Marienbad* (Further Other Book Works, 2016) and for their friendship.

Thank you to so many friends, teachers, mentors, and guides for conversation, advice, kindness, and care: Mary Jo Bang, Mildred Barya, Teresa Carmody, Carolina Ebeid, Donna Beth Ellard, Graham Foust, Brandi Homan, Laird Hunt, Jennifer Kronovet, Nithin Manayath, Vivek Narayanan, Nathanaël, Jeffrey Pethybridge, Carl Phillips, Allan Popa, Bin Ramke, Selah Saterstrom, Eleni Sikelianos, Sumant Srivathsan, Sridala Swami, and Michael Joseph Walsh.

Thank you so very much, Kazim Ali, Lindsey Boldt, Stephen Motika, and Margaret Tedesco, for shaping and shepherding this book to completion.

Lastly, thank you to my parents, Francis and Margaret Machado, who are wonderful.

ADITI MACHADO is an Indian poet. Previous works include the chapbook *Route: Marienbad* and her translation of Farid Tali's *Prosopopoeia*. She is the poetry editor of *Asymptote*, a journal of translation.

NIGHTBOAT BOOKS

Nightboat Books, a nonprofit organization, seeks to develop audiences for writers whose work resists convention and transcends boundaries. We publish books rich with poignancy, intelligence, and risk. Please visit our website, www.nightboat.org, to learn about our titles and how you can support our future publications.

The following individuals have supported the publication of this book. We thank them for their generosity and commitment to the mission of Nightboat Books:

Elizabeth Motika
Benjamin Taylor

In addition, this book has been made possible, in part, by grants from the National Endowment for the Arts and the New York State Council on the Arts Literature Program.